Carapace

CARAPACE

Poems by Henry Kanabus

Acknowledgements: Some of these poems originally appeared (in slightly different form) in *Big Sky, Brilliant Corners, The (Chicago) Reader, Milk Quarterly, Mati, Out There, Here It Is,* and *Stone Wind.*

Special thanks to Peter Kostakis for his assistance in the compilation of this manuscript (and)

Loving gratitude to Amy Beth Golden for innumerable suggestions, continued support, and hours of hard work.

The Yellow Press
2394 Blue Island
Chicago, IL. 60608

Library of Congress Cataloging in Publication Data
Kanabus, Henry, 1949—
    Carapace : Poems.

    I. Title.
PS3561.A457C3   811'.5'4   77-13815
ISBN 0-916328-09-0 pbk.

Yellow Press books are distributed by *SBD: Small Press Distribution,* 1636 Ocean View Ave., Kensington, CA. 94707. Please order from them.

Cover photos and design by Mike Tappin.

Publication of this book has been partially supported by a grant from The Illinois Arts Council, an agency of the state.

CONTENTS

SONG

His hand introduces
a spool of ballerinas

The black mane flies
and wings bend

The blind wind
fuses on the two lane.

GASOLINE HARVEST

She entices with solidarity
the blue green windows
    of the truck

And the wheels lock passing
avatars of white sleep

She is deliciously sane
casting only minor glances
at familiars
    abounding in air

As with the tremulous
day watch
peril grimaces (weary with joy)
spent with stars.

THE SKULL . FLOCCULENT

Cicadas construct in the bones
of his face

rag huts and wicker palaces

applying to a sturdy tooth
a patina of luxuriant eyes
apart from avarice

      in colors of kerosene

and hover obdurately
within the dome

of the human continent.

PILLARS OF STEEPLE WINE

A particle of nonchalance
fastidious in impulse

whining in maturation

approaching yet another
oblivious dawn.

With her languid mouth and crinoline
she is extant

covers the bed in a lisp

She is perfection
        with a broken tooth.

THE PEWTER VASE

Believing in another season
revealing wings to small
                          animals

          and claws to the sky

               Your pharmaceutical precaution
shattered by the window rock
hurled in envy

Lace will document (eventually)
the myriad lives you've lead
to this conclusion:

          The ugly women
          pursue the ugly men

          I am entranced by rails
saying little to the moon.

DANCE POEM

Grandma is so intelligent
her incisor teeth
               remain diligent

after 14 years
in the sod.

CHIMES

It is a calm yellow sun
that cajoles the air

                to vanish

You inhale fibers
of the dog

and a wiser night has fallen
from the circus

sky   onto the dust
                of a thousand saws.

It is a woman who wakes you
all your life.

SECOND MAGNITUDE

With her scissoring fiercely through the
star charts, I half expect the eastern
hemisphere to erupt in comets of protest.
On the other half, I expect my best straight
razor, with the tortoise shell casing and
the insignia of the wolf cult, to be dull
in the morning and mean and reticent for
my silence.
She has successfully regrouped the stars
of Orion into a semblance of our landlord.
By the first of the month, she says, he
will fold over the horizon and begrudge
the tenants of Antwerp.

SPRING FASHION

Have you seen her costume
(Mucho chic)

A chiffon number
with wrought iron sequins
buttressed by giant penises

It isn't designed for
        walking

In fact no motion at all
is feasible

She just stands in this
creation, writhing her fingers
looking incredible.

POEM WITH SNOW AND SATIN

The snow descends the spiral
tendrils of the pine
easing toward the frozen earth
like a meek avalanche

And there . you discern through the glass
a woman
whose blouse (she wears a greatcoat)
you know is satin or blue sky silk
by the way she purses

her lips to the packets of winter dust
striking her face   her eyes
                         striking her face

She furrows on the burdened concrete
lines of departure
follow her
        gaze to her spine
strung like a bow . taut with wire.

A HAT FOR DASHIELL

The wings of the servants
and forest hats.

Oh *romantic perigee* how am I
to salvage even your circus tent

The clowns have escaped with the best
of the rigging
                        and the geek
has turned
his eyes on the Great Zildaff

Pony me to Rome or south
St. Louis

Even the bride who gave me children
is grafting hats
onto the rubes
                        faster than

I can sling them
onto the rack.

NIGHT BEHIND THE REVEREND'S DESK

For you she is many . is extraordinary
commandeering beauty
with every glance

The leaf like presence
                of your vigilante

obvious in abattoirs
accorded a jubilant day

For you she is woven
and lays on the dais in wait.

.

Adramelech shouted . the
only voice operative
        'the house is in flames
            secure the wanton'

And you fold it then
in the whiskey of your body
    in your ambient skin

waking in the ancient morning
looking for him . his name

The hair and the mirror
the chill of the floor
when you came.

FULGURITE

(for Amy Beth Golden)

It is not that ruminating child
you purport to occupy
that entices the abject
carnivals of lethargy
seething like wayfarers
in my ocean spine

Your furnace stipulates
coarse packets of winter brine
A message follows:

Gazing your heart
returns and is burgeoned
with tallow   A window reclines
content with silver
Talismans of pine
        endeavor to harness your mirror

They cannot

I am oceaneyed and river
carried   You are
raven haired festooned
with miracles
Talons emerge from the sky.

THE PARAPET

In the force of a second he
realizes there is a bounty
on beautiful hats
            and gregarious children

Hoisting his bell-book and his lariat

sketching maps of infamous
accuracy
the gadfly lays its eggs

in his third eye and he
is blinded to magick

.

The carnival heals
and fills the day with green things

brocading land
for tranquil ceremonies.

FANTASIA ON THE CONTINENT

Very few days remain.

I slashed him quickly
(would have killed him)

the razor clenched
the victory tremulous

       with ivory hands

Secure in the placid gravity
of death he spoke of his daughter

a youngish wife

Lizards droned about
the still yellow hemisphere.

THE STRONG WIND

Musicale.

Damn the wind.   It moves me

honing the structures of the continent
into spires of arcanum

Amber in the dayflow
                encasing limbs & necklaces
in reliquary silence
                (further than love)

It has glimpsed
the light of evening
native to this region of level ground

Forcing the window
entering the house

        touching everything.

STREAKS

With songs and arctic vision
given opulence

          and a careful predilection
to the urgency
of the affair
                    he watches
                    the white woman

precipitate to clouds of thunder
black

As leather falls
to the beaten earth

her hair

lashes onto his chest
and she is silent there.

FOUND: A COPPER TRUNK

Paraguay. You encounter
a harvest of skeletal vestments

an appurtenance of burgeoning
saint hair & bacchant letters

Is it simple anguish you detest
The mannequin falters
                (questions the guests)

Charles Henri Ford begs
silence and will not eat.

ACCORDANCE

'Certainties are arrived at only on foot.'
The darkening road permeates his right eye,
his left chatters like a tympany in which
lacewings are imprisoned. He sings to his
nurse. She has kept him in bed for over
a decade. Long since, he has ceased calling
her his muse. She brings him coffee and cake,
a small boat, and a fork to eat the fish
with some enchantment for the lake it had
crept in.

THE ACCESS

you've grown to fire
delicately

The archer (acquainted with brilliance)
inhabits a desperate vanity

Lace becomes an adjunct
to flame

An error in tribal delineations
places the magician
in the homes of the mad

It is pride not wealth
that traces disparate feathers

on the white arena
of his skin

Easy to see how starlight
becomes deadly
      when you walk with him.

THE WHITE VASE BROKEN

Brittle encouragement
sugared in the night
            with Spanish women

lacquered with concrete
island passion

and visions of nail polish
stolen at drugstores

Cutting the street like jig saws
and cadmium fright

        (telling the time)

addressing the same god
she has driven
                to the end
of opera

Worn in the healing the old
shoes
        bitch for love

I return with bands of soil
eager to bury
your bracelet limb
in my jacket

Ridden with songs
                of you.

TINCTURE OF MALINDA FAYE

The Chinese umbrella
you held . a marriage
on the next block

Straw kites and pin spokes
the nature of fire
cracker mache'

Black cat so green with
Li Po characters
                    dancing

for the sun
    god you say

She bought (for a nickel)
a roll of caps

The blind druggist
with digital ardor
gave you the chart

            'detonation of many
             numbers is certain'

The claws of young animals
assume arboreal functions
in lieu of autumn
                        leaving

brittle shoulders
on your copper dress.

HORSE LATITUDES

When they have sailed
for many distances
they are humbled by the vast horizon

In their packs
of numerology . they are favored

Creatures of the trade winds
call them vipers
            visionaries

charlatans of oceans

Near those lines again
we perceive great fear in the horses.

THE DAY PATCH CONTINUUM

1.

The *time traveler* disengages his shoestring

He has logged gates and iron timber
He has accepted this day

In the Coffin City he appears
to anger inmates
                    he retreats to further
                    ventures on the hill

Nightwind reaches the glib sun at twilight

It contorts the vision
of the *traveler* to spatial purity

Vengeance is wreaked upon the throat
        with blind foot thrusts

                Wisdom is concealed
and waits for morning songs

.

The cartwheel princess arrives
wearing nothing

She convolutes the clouds
     in regions of high urgency
     calling by name the wisps of water life

Her quickening glance
darts to planetary boundaries

                    She marries young
and keeps her eyes in spite.

2.

In his ancestral garage
(decored in ashen clarity)
he stores bark carvings of oak and cedar

Vigilant carriages conceived in stone
                              hang from the rooftop
Jars of blight
rest on many shelves

It is well that he remembers morning

its red light bleeding
breaking the day

        . . . the coffers of sound
sealing the feeding fire
the white moon

                shrieking down.

3.

The *time traveler*
    stood in the foothills
    of a great land

His arctic hands left winter
on cleaved sandstone

His apparition
shouldered all his bones and tendrils
hollowing his chest in the insect moon

white time white time
flows in a serpentine gait
                like great rivers

enticing the dead with molecules of mad configuration

Electrons in quick valence patterns
of 3 & 9
converge on the tarot builder

    He too is a *time traveler*
weary of violence and dread

his eyes are a constant reminder
                he is afraid

He can see himself at the mouth of an ugly winter

                he is afraid.

4.

She comes to him

                with a tarnished dance
                at the heat of a whisper

Her writhing hands
assume a distant gesture of despair

He attempts to hear her voice
compressing the oceans of air

. . . he cannot hear her.

5.

Silver her breast is
in the morning   with warm leaves
                      and mint nipples

Stranger to mountains
her eyes are fire in pine forests
beneath the settling
                                        sky

She is holding the carapace of the world
glistening like kerosene

Time becomes an anecdote of pure color

Rain stretches precise constellations
into running wounds.

EVENING WITH PARASOLS

Beth.

I am not gauged by your passion
yet feel a verging on delight
when you afford me visions
sans cloth

.

         The mill of repose
weaves
an article of such blind wonder
as even to the dark
they sense

the scent of color you signify

.

I fear little but the tinner
and his tympanic hammer

rending with precise concussion
the fabric of your night sleeve .

A ruby drops.

HOBKIN'S DEBILITATING MOOD

Swagger in your pink
sweater
     and your gable stole

The fact that you are ectogenous
has little to do with your sweet
ass . blue dress

Necromancy takes its place

assumes an erection of
incredible duration

     (years pass)
It is silver
that occupies the coffers
you possess

the moon

shelters fragments of the sky
from your gaze.

CLEATS

Aphasia.

I would like to see you

       well bred
       well defined

An illusion occurs

You sew yourself up (and)
paste yourself with

criminal types.

THE TIME CLASP OF ST. AGNES' DREAM

Fierce angels mounted
women in the service
    of the sun

           Gunlight shouted
'cross the river of the storm

There were fine gentlemen
bleeding from the knees

There were elegant thieves
killed in context

Drifters of the sudden source
fastened at the feet

She enters
        fleshed in silk

and bound in silence.

PLEASANCE & PENETRALIA (1932)

Buddha in the opium den.

His 'big baby'
form hangs grotesquely
from the wooden tier

its boards
resinous with dreams—
a ladder of searching

voyaging skulls
a pilgrimage of hollow eyes

the fog deepens

A caterpillar churns
at the borders of recognition

'Another of your oriental tricks'
says the boy archaeologist.

GAMBLER (1944)

The onset precluded heavy leaps

Fortune and the Puerto Rican in
the window . you might
amuse yourself
with just such   frozen
clocks on the photo sphere
your favorite hour jack-knifed
onto your face

There is a wisdom in with-
holding

In four locks he appears.

OPIUM SONG (1893)

The horse and rider

galloped underwater

in slow liquid strides

The chinaman's long black

hair moved like seaweed

in a rising tide

THE STONE PERCH

An obelisk of light
deepens its wing

into stone
the claws rend

into spines
of plumage

screech
owls the partition

the hawk bends
black kites

descend to branches

THE BOY

          Beautiful you can become

as telegraph and winter masks

assume the days of children's

          alley ways . departures

from clothing held

securely like a bird of prey

within the brittle

                    skull only

to maim

to rend viciously breath

from the belly

          If only . . . Hey, there's

Jimmy . Jimmy the wren's

beak!

THE CENTIPEDE

Stretched with the lamp
in a graceless day
appointed foreign
            emissary of joy
the attic
rings the inconsequential cartridge
that love forgave
loads a precise deity
into the furnace
            ganglion and knotted
blade

Oh, common law anger.

POEM

Wonderful kettle fish
exclusively for fund raising.

AFTER THOUGHT

1.

There is time he said
a white sound chirrups
the ear fills

red cobblestones
white wheels of wood
    and iron

a darling child
green hills
yes . sunlight

2.

In the night
her skin is
visibly white

crystals of snow
flow gently
warm her breast

a tide of silver
pleases
her temperament

graceful is she
that bends
her quiet body.

BELOVED CHANTAGE

There is a fragrance
in her eyes
            compelling the poet's fingers
to her breasts . . . heirlooms
of white gold
cold to the touch
        of strangers   I
to her lover warm
to the taste . . . her nipples
like summer metal
long in the sun

BROADWAY SUN

The position of variable
stars and the cage

latticed blue truck
sparkle in the morning

when the rain hits up
against the trellis

.

Clamor in the petite
locomotion of her

butterfly hips
singing (almost) a song

of ingenious adventure
with salt like parchment

on her pallid lips.

BATTLE FIGURINES

In the forest folk's bestiary
tattooed star charts
resemble ancestral dreams

Yet it matters very little
One concedes or amputates.

The real concern
lies with coronary
battle shields

One secretly knows
of madrigal armor for the heart

wrought in Spanish silver
filigreed with ivory

worn like love.

FRAZETTA ON THE CRUX

The crucified hilltop sculptor
spoke with a mouth full
of blood and Copenhagen
fine 'chaw' mixture

Cartaphilus said
                'the oratory
was extraordinary' as he spat
into an abysmal spittoon

Golgotha staggered
carved into a phoenix of blue fire

Rage engaged his five fingers
talons entered his eyes.

THE GLASS FURNACE

Aged . almost mummified
the concordat of armor
slashes through the battlements
of winter wait

He holds the pen
perched like an eagle
angered by the social graces
collapsing with mad laughter

If he is fed
    he will die of bloated gratitude

He will hunger

calling it the last
white feast of solitude.

THE TALL GRASS

A blanket for your
warm

       A pretty dollar
       for your shoe to be
       perfect again

Walk to the moon
where the cask lies open

       and the hooves

hold
antlers laden with rain.

AMULET AND SINEW

Belly of your target
        speared with white emotion

I came on your tits

You enchanted
bus drivers to let you smoke

THE DEAD CHAPERONE

The porcelain pig
anesthetized by volition

flew like the Styx and returned
like a beetle on a string

She sleeps with her time
and her moonstone rings

How precise her wings
is yet uncertain.

COBBLE PROMENADE

A cloud mustache
and sheet guns

The incredible walking
turtle

Sky ships
painted

      Flare guns
      crimson

The laugh of the
      giant sunflower

The yodel of the siren
on a sunday

HEIRLOOM (1895)

Spring in the park
she walks around
the lagoon
A water flower rests
    on the mirror

She speaks to a willow
sings of a lover
The green breaks open
                    into deeper green

Silence of the water
assured in liquid

secured in this
            your portrait.

SUNSHADE

Having no lips
secures her face with paint

a pink thing . with
shoulders like a wren

an insect's green wing
flutters from her eye
                        escaping

serrating hair she
purchases
                old pistols

placing in her hand
the perfect flood.

THE FELT HAT (BLOCKED)

A big table hat in the rain
with coffin satin clothing
the silver ware . the stitches

Cap storms by the spacious
meat . bleeding it
supremely

       speaking to it
calling it fibrous
love unhooved

cutting with its pincer teeth
blue veins bleat
(burnished and branded)

the black goat sleeps
and will awaken
skewered by her foot.

POTION FOR THE SYBARITES

What do you will
my lady footprint

Perhaps the sun
will seed before your eyes

                        or rain
will fill the hollow of your heart

The river of your enmity
may turn from you or it may not

I will say it for you

Calliopies and nightweeds
steep this river
deep in magick

As the night we loved
on its sloping banks

clinging with young skin
to the timid clay
                under thorn trees

lover . do not touch
          the thorn trees

they are shelter
and their jagged leaves pertain.

THE IRON FOREST

Be so still (young woman)
that a hawk

could alight on your shoulder
and mistake you

for a region
deep within a forest

of dark elms

at noon

She is buying an umbrella
from the morphine cartel
and taking his advice

to her room.

THE GAUGE

Odd that the specimen
    you considered

should resolve itself
    to be
    yourself / as another

wanted you.

THE WHIZZBANG CHART

There is a casual
myth to this .   like Laurina

in the morning when she
strips to a carapace

of glass then strips further.

It is not so much a sacrament
but a glacial feat
                (that which)

melts
to the core of an unexpected jewel

and is *still* marvelous.

NIGHTSCAPE

Faltering in this season
of reluctant gloves

an apostle of the grain belt
has secured four notes
of suicide

from your porcelain pocket
and will not relent

.

He has brought you
silver in a cyclone truck

and has painted
the wings of his falcon
a dark red

Gasoline cats attack
the dressmaker's fortress

eager to ascend.

THE HOMUNCULUS SCORNED

Is it because you loved
the broken horse . the flying
horse that carried

        (far from you, baby)

your turgid eye
your reckless waist

Wondrously you recalled
the sapience on his shoulder
and his great beard growing

as the moon survived
the winged eclipse

.

A figure in the sand
                at a distance

difficult to accept

As a child you regained
your sight and saw

everything.

VIOLET OPTICS

For weeks I have not seen you

   (wonder if still I love you)

In a younger day
the darkening sky
     stirred my sensibilities
     like Gothic architecture

Now I question
the merits of courtesy

brood over
     constricting possibilities

I have spoken to the chair
It disagrees.

POEM

And with that you hold
your diamond

ring to his lap
and part your hair

in perfect
hemispheres of black

loosing the sails
that could be the wings

your child remembers
when speaking of lamps.

THE SCYTHE

The wind accounted for all
it had shattered
                    (night-dancing
in lace prints of bone)

We confuse its wisdom
with the anger of cats . both

lay large upon the wheat

We realize the urgency and notify
the heliotrope

            It is waving its arms
in a thousand different parodies.

Other Yellow Press Books:

Red Wagon—Poems by Ted Berrigan

paperback ISBN 0-916328-01-5 $3.00
cloth   ISBN 0-916328-05-8 $7.95

Straight—Poems 1971-1975 by Richard Friedman

paperback ISBN 0-916328-00-7 $2.00

Alice Ordered Me to Be Made—Poems 1975
                                    by Alice Notley

paperback ISBN 0-916328-02-3 $2.50
cloth   ISBN 0-916328-06-6 $6.95

The Grand Et Cet'ra—Poems by Barry Schechter

paperback ISBN 0-916328-07-4 $2.50

15 Chicago Poets (Ted Berrigan, Walter Bradford, Gwendolyn Brooks, Paul Carroll, Maxine Chernoff, Richard Friedman, Paul Hoover, Angela Jackson, Henry Kanabus, Peter Kostakis, Art Lange, Haki R. Madhubuti (Don L. Lee), Alice Notley, Darlene Pearlstein, Barry Schechter)—Edited by Richard Friedman, Peter Kostakis, Darlene Pearlstein; 2nd printing

paperback ISBN 0-916328-03-1 $3.00
cloth   ISBN 0-916328-04-X $7.95

The Hat Issue (Contributions from Marion Brown, Robert Creeley, Russell Edson, Joseph Jarman, Erica Jong, Alex Katz, Etheridge Knight, Kenneth Koch, Richard Kostelanetz, Oliver Lake, John Lennon, Jay Lynch, Thomas McGuane, Paul Metcalf, Alice Notley, Claes Oldenburg, Yoko Ono, James Schuyler, James Tate, Anne Waldman et al., *Milk Quarterly 11 & 12*)—Edited by Peter Kostakis

paperback ISBN 0-916328-08-2 $3.00

Yellow Press books are distributed by *SBD: Small Press Distribution*, 1636 Ocean View Ave., Kensington, CA. 94707
Please order from them.

By the author:

FLOODLIGHTS (Poems 1971-1973)

Typeset in 12 point Garamond by Barrett Watten
at The West Coast Print Center, Inc., Berkeley, CA.
Printed in the USA by Braun-Brumfield.
26 copies are lettered A-Z
and signed by the author.